First Science

Build it Strong!

W9-BJK-261

Editorial planning: Serpentine Editorial
Scientific consultant: Dr. J.J.M. Rowe

Designed by The R & B Partnership
Illustrator: David Anstey
Photographer: Peter Millard

Additional photographs:
Chris Fairclough Colour Library 8, 18;
G. Ziesler/Bruce Coleman 10;
Leonard Lee Rue/Bruce Coleman 11;
Julian Rowe 13;
Eye Ubiquitous 14;
The Hutchison Library 20;
ZEFA 22;
David Woodfall/NHPA 28.

Library of Congress Cataloging-in-Publication Data

Rowe, Julian.
   Build it strong! / by Julian Rowe and Molly Perham.
     p.   cm. — (First science)
   Includes index.
   ISBN 0-516-08138-1
   1. Structural engineering—Juvenile literature. [1. Structural engineering—
Experiments. 2. Experiments.] I. Perham, Molly. II. Title. III. Series: First science
(Chicago, Ill.)
TA634.R67 1994
624'.1—dc20   94-16941
                                                                     CIP
                                                                      AC

First Science

Build it Strong!

Julian Rowe
and Molly Perham

CP CHILDRENS PRESS®

CHICAGO

Contents

 SAFETY WARNING
Activities marked with this symbol require the
presence and help of an adult.

Build it!

Build a tower with wooden blocks.
Can you make it strong and steady?

Or will your tower fall down easily?

Bricklaying

Have you ever seen a house being built?
These bricks are made of clay. They were
baked in a very hot oven, or kiln, until they
became hard and strong.

Builders use mortar to join bricks together.
Mortar is a mixture of sand,
cement, and water.
When it dries, it
becomes hard
and strong. This
girl is using
mortar to build
a brick wall.

Animal builders

Many birds use clay or mud to build their nests. The mud dries in the sun and becomes hard and firm.

The rufous oven bird in South America makes a round nest of mud, grass, and hair.

Beavers use their sharp teeth to cut down trees. They build a large dome-shaped home of branches and twigs.

The spaces between the branches are filled with mud. A beaver's home is called a lodge.

Firm foundations

A building needs to stand on a firm foundation. If you build on soft sand, the building sinks and may fall over.

Laying a block underneath the building spreads out the weight. Then the building stands firm.

Before a house is built, a foundation is laid
by pouring concrete into deep trenches.

Roofs

A building needs a strong roof to protect it from the weather. How many different roof shapes can you see in this picture?

Large buildings sometimes have a dome-shaped roof.

The weight of the roof is spread out over the sloping sides of the dome.

Materials: Two large cereal boxes, a book, and two rulers.

1. Stand the cereal boxes a few inches apart to make walls. Open the book in the middle to make a roof.

Investigate roofs

2. Can you balance the roof on top of the walls? The weight of the roof forces the walls apart.

3. Now lay the rulers across the cereal boxes.

Can you balance the roof now?

Strong shapes

It is easy to squash a cardboard tube by squeezing it in the middle. It is very difficult to squash it by pressing on the ends!

These boxes have
strong corners. They
can be stacked on
top of each other.

A stepladder makes
a triangle shape
with the floor.

The ladder is
strong enough
to stand on.

Pylons

Pylons carry heavy electric cables across the country. These tall towers have to be very strong so that winds do not blow them down.

The tower structure is made of thin strips of steel joined together and crossed in a special pattern.

Can you see any strong shapes?

Make a pylon

Materials: Drinking straws, tape, and scissors.

1. Cut short pieces of tape. Wrap them around the ends of the straws to make a square shape.

2. Now start to build your power tower.

What shape makes your tower strong?

Carrying weight

The shape of an arch makes it very strong. The weight above is spread outward down the curves.

Strong eggs

Materials: Four eggshells, masking tape, scissors, and some books.

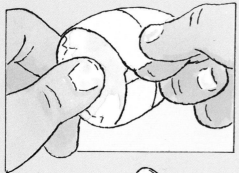

1. Put masking tape around the middle of each eggshell.

2. Carefully cut around the eggshell through the masking tape.

3. Place the eggshells cut side down.

4. Put a book on top of them.

How many books can you pile up before the shells break?

Bridges

Bridges are made in different shapes and of many different materials.

They can be made from stone, wood, metal, or even rope. Suspension bridges are held up by strong steel cables.

How many different bridge shapes
can you make?

Test the strength of your bridge by
placing weights in the middle.

Traveling light

Some structures are strong but also light. Tents provide a warm and dry place to sleep when you are traveling. They are light and easy to carry.

Why do tents have to be pegged firmly into the ground?

Make a tent

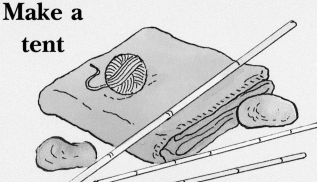

Materials: A long pole, four short sticks, strong string, an old blanket, and some stones.

1. Tie the ends of two sticks together with string. Do the same with the other two.

2. Make the frame of the tent by tying the pole to the sticks. Use string to hold the frame firm.

3. Put the blanket over the frame. Use stones to hold it in place.

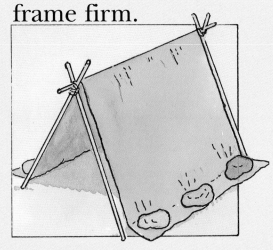

Can you make another tent with a different shape?

25

Testing materials

Builders must know the strength of the materials they use. One way to test the strength of materials is to try to break them. Paper, plastic, and aluminum foil are being tested above. Which material do you think is the strongest?

Blocks of wood are often glued together to make strong structures. This boy and girl are testing the strength of their glue.

Acid rain

Poisonous gases from cars and power plants mix with rain and make it acid rain.

Stone is a strong building material, but acid rain makes it so weak that it crumbles away.

You can see how the sculpture on this old building has been damaged by acid rain.

How acid rain works

Materials: A lump of chalk, vinegar, and a small plastic bowl.

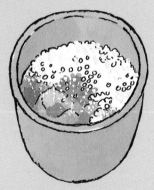

1. Put some pieces of chalk in the bowl.

2. Pour enough vinegar over the chalk to cover it.

What happens to the chalk?

Vinegar is an acid, like acid rain. Chalk is like the stone used for building.

Think about... building

Some buildings have a dome-shaped roof. A chain held at each end forms a curve. This is the best shape for a dome.

Coats of varnish protect wood from the weather. Varnish makes the wood waterproof.

Bricks can be laid in many different ways. Bricks are placed on top of each other in different patterns called "bonds."

Some different bonds are shown here.

Here are some of the materials that builders use.

Which of them can you find in your house?